INTERIOR DESIGN

NOTEBOOK

Designer:

By The Bockborn

PROJECT

Sheet title

Client

Date

Drawn by

Notes

Details

Materials

Floor

Wall

Colors

Lights

Furniture

Decoration

Overall mood

Mood board: Material samples/ Details/ Drafting

PROJECT	
Sheet title	
Client	
Date	
Drawn by	
Notes	

Details	
Materials	
Floor	
Wall	
Colors	
Lights	
Furniture	
Decoration	
Overall mood	

Mood board: Material samples/ Details/ Drafting

PROJECT	
Sheet title	
Client	
Date	
Drawn by	
Notes	

Details	
Materials	
Floor	
Wall	
Colors	
Lights	
Furniture	
Decoration	
Overall mood	

PROJECT

Sheet title	
Client	
Date	
Drawn by	
Notes	

Details	
Materials	
Floor	
Wall	
Colors	
Lights	
Furniture	
Decoration	
Overall mood	

Mood board: Material samples/ Details/ Drafting

PROJECT

Sheet title

Client

Date

Drawn by

Notes

Details

Materials

Floor

Wall

Colors

Lights

Furniture

Decoration

Overall mood

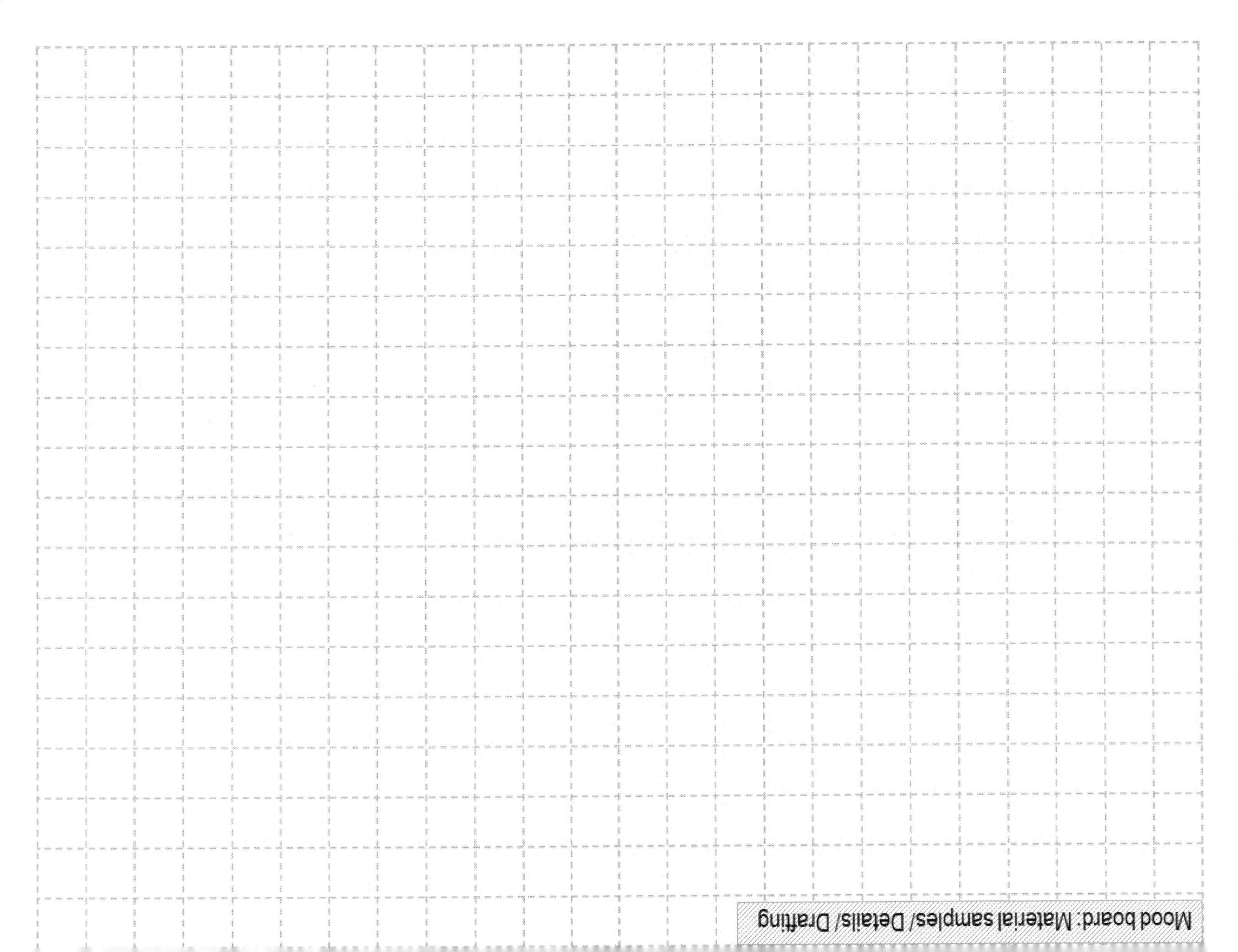

Mood board: Material samples/ Details/ Drafting

PROJECT

Sheet title	
Client	
Date	
Drawn by	
Notes	

Details	
Materials	
Floor	
Wall	
Colors	
Lights	
Furniture	
Decoration	
Overall mood	

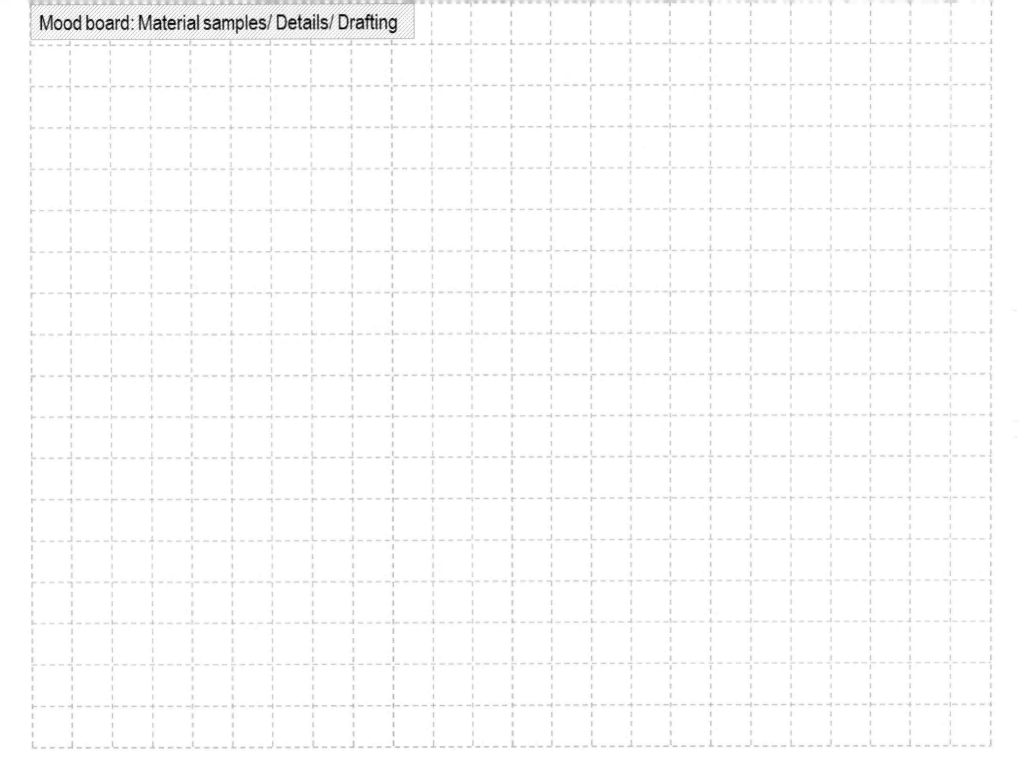

Mood board: Material samples/ Details/ Drafting

PROJECT

Sheet title

Client

Date

Drawn by

Notes

Details

Materials

Floor

Wall

Colors

Lights

Furniture

Decoration

Overall mood

PROJECT		Details	
Sheet title		Materials	
Client		Floor	
Date		Wall	
Drawn by		Colors	
Notes		Lights	
		Furniture	
		Decoration	
		Overall mood	

PROJECT

Sheet title	
Client	
Date	
Drawn by	
Notes	

Details	
Materials	
Floor	
Wall	
Colors	
Lights	
Furniture	
Decoration	
Overall mood	

Mood board: Material samples/ Details/ Drafting

PROJECT

Sheet title	
Client	
Date	
Drawn by	
Notes	

Details	
Materials	
Floor	
Wall	
Colors	
Lights	
Furniture	
Decoration	
Overall mood	

Mood board: Material samples/ Details/ Drafting

PROJECT

Sheet title

Client

Date

Drawn by

Notes

Details

Materials

Floor

Wall

Colors

Lights

Furniture

Decoration

Overall
mood

PROJECT

Sheet title	
Client	
Date	
Drawn by	
Notes	

Details	
Materials	
Floor	
Wall	
Colors	
Lights	
Furniture	
Decoration	
Overall mood	

PROJECT	
Sheet title	
Client	
Date	
Drawn by	
Notes	

Details	
Materials	
Floor	
Wall	
Colors	
Lights	
Furniture	
Decoration	
Overall mood	

PROJECT		Details	
Sheet title		Materials	
Client		Floor	
Date		Wall	
Drawn by		Colors	
Notes		Lights	
		Furniture	
		Decoration	
		Overall mood	

Mood board: Material samples/ Details/ Drafting

PROJECT		Details	
Sheet title		Materials	
Client		Floor	
Date		Wall	
Drawn by		Colors	
Notes		Lights	
		Furniture	
		Decoration	
		Overall mood	

Mood board: Material samples/ Details/ Drafting

PROJECT	
Sheet title	
Client	
Date	
Drawn by	
Notes	

Details	
Materials	
Floor	
Wall	
Colors	
Lights	
Furniture	
Decoration	
Overall mood	

Mood board: Material samples/ Details/ Drafting

PROJECT

Sheet title

Client

Date

Drawn by

Notes

Details

Materials

Floor

Wall

Colors

Lights

Furniture

Decoration

Overall mood

Mood board: Material samples/ Details/ Drafting

PROJECT

Sheet title	
Client	
Date	
Drawn by	
Notes	

Details	
Materials	
Floor	
Wall	
Colors	
Lights	
Furniture	
Decoration	
Overall mood	

PROJECT

Sheet title

Client

Date

Drawn by

Notes

Details

Materials

Floor

Wall

Colors

Lights

Furniture

Decoration

Overall
mood

Mood board: Material samples/ Details/ Drafting

PROJECT	
Sheet title	
Client	
Date	
Drawn by	
Notes	

Details	
Materials	
Floor	
Wall	
Colors	
Lights	
Furniture	
Decoration	
Overall mood	

Mood board: Material samples/ Details/ Drafting

PROJECT

Sheet title

Client

Date

Drawn by

Notes

Details

Materials

Floor

Wall

Colors

Lights

Furniture

Decoration

Overall mood

PROJECT		Details	
Sheet title		Materials	
Client		Floor	
Date		Wall	
Drawn by		Colors	
Notes		Lights	
		Furniture	
		Decoration	
		Overall mood	

Mood board: Material samples/ Details/ Drafting

PROJECT

Sheet title	
Client	
Date	
Drawn by	
Notes	

Details

Materials	
Floor	
Wall	
Colors	
Lights	
Furniture	
Decoration	
Overall mood	

Mood board: Material samples/ Details/ Drafting

PROJECT		Details	
Sheet title		Materials	
Client		Floor	
Date		Wall	
Drawn by		Colors	
Notes		Lights	
		Furniture	
		Decoration	
		Overall mood	

PROJECT		Details	
Sheet title		Materials	
Client		Floor	
Date		Wall	
Drawn by		Colors	
Notes		Lights	
		Furniture	
		Decoration	
		Overall mood	

PROJECT	
Sheet title	
Client	
Date	
Drawn by	
Notes	

Details	
Materials	
Floor	
Wall	
Colors	
Lights	
Furniture	
Decoration	
Overall mood	

PROJECT	
Sheet title	
Client	
Date	
Drawn by	
Notes	

Details	
Materials	
Floor	
Wall	
Colors	
Lights	
Furniture	
Decoration	
Overall mood	

Mood board: Material samples/ Details/ Drafting

PROJECT	
Sheet title	
Client	
Date	
Drawn by	
Notes	

Details	
Materials	
Floor	
Wall	
Colors	
Lights	
Furniture	
Decoration	
Overall mood	

Mood board: Material samples/ Details/ Drafting

PROJECT	
Sheet title	
Client	
Date	
Drawn by	
Notes	

Details	
Materials	
Floor	
Wall	
Colors	
Lights	
Furniture	
Decoration	
Overall mood	

PROJECT	
Sheet title	
Client	
Date	
Drawn by	
Notes	

Details	
Materials	
Floor	
Wall	
Colors	
Lights	
Furniture	
Decoration	
Overall mood	

Mood board: Material samples/ Details/ Drafting

PROJECT		Details	
Sheet title		Materials	
Client		Floor	
Date		Wall	
Drawn by		Colors	
Notes		Lights	
		Furniture	
		Decoration	
		Overall mood	

Mood board: Material samples/ Details/ Drafting

PROJECT		Details	
Sheet title		Materials	
Client		Floor	
Date		Wall	
Drawn by		Colors	
Notes		Lights	
		Furniture	
		Decoration	
		Overall mood	

Mood board: Material samples/ Details/ Drafting

PROJECT

Sheet title	
Client	
Date	
Drawn by	
Notes	

Details	
Materials	
Floor	
Wall	
Colors	
Lights	
Furniture	
Decoration	
Overall mood	

PROJECT

Sheet title	
Client	
Date	
Drawn by	
Notes	

Details	
Materials	
Floor	
Wall	
Colors	
Lights	
Furniture	
Decoration	
Overall mood	

Mood board: Material samples/ Details/ Drafting

PROJECT	
Sheet title	
Client	
Date	
Drawn by	
Notes	

Details	
Materials	
Floor	
Wall	
Colors	
Lights	
Furniture	
Decoration	
Overall mood	

Mood board: Material samples/ Details/ Drafting

PROJECT	
Sheet title	
Client	
Date	
Drawn by	
Notes	

Details	
Materials	
Floor	
Wall	
Colors	
Lights	
Furniture	
Decoration	
Overall mood	

PROJECT	
Sheet title	
Client	
Date	
Drawn by	
Notes	

Details	
Materials	
Floor	
Wall	
Colors	
Lights	
Furniture	
Decoration	
Overall mood	

Mood board: Material samples/ Details/ Drafting

PROJECT		Details	
Sheet title		Materials	
Client		Floor	
Date		Wall	
Drawn by		Colors	
Notes		Lights	
		Furniture	
		Decoration	
		Overall mood	

Mood board: Material samples/ Details/ Drafting

PROJECT	
Sheet title	
Client	
Date	
Drawn by	
Notes	

Details	
Materials	
Floor	
Wall	
Colors	
Lights	
Furniture	
Decoration	
Overall mood	

Mood board: Material samples/ Details/ Drafting

PROJECT	
Sheet title	
Client	
Date	
Drawn by	
Notes	

Details	
Materials	
Floor	
Wall	
Colors	
Lights	
Furniture	
Decoration	
Overall mood	

PROJECT	
Sheet title	
Client	
Date	
Drawn by	
Notes	

Details	
Materials	
Floor	
Wall	
Colors	
Lights	
Furniture	
Decoration	
Overall mood	

PROJECT		Details	
Sheet title		Materials	
Client		Floor	
Date		Wall	
Drawn by		Colors	
Notes		Lights	
		Furniture	
		Decoration	
		Overall mood	

Mood board: Material samples/ Details/ Drafting

PROJECT		Details	
Sheet title		Materials	
Client		Floor	
Date		Wall	
Drawn by		Colors	
Notes		Lights	
		Furniture	
		Decoration	
		Overall mood	

Mood board: Material samples/ Details/ Drafting

PROJECT		Details	
Sheet title		Materials	
Client		Floor	
Date		Wall	
Drawn by		Colors	
Notes		Lights	
		Furniture	
		Decoration	
		Overall mood	

Mood board: Material samples/ Details/ Drafting

PROJECT

Sheet title

Client

Date

Drawn by

Notes

Details

Materials

Floor

Wall

Colors

Lights

Furniture

Decoration

Overall
mood

Mood board: Material samples/ Details/ Drafting

PROJECT	
Sheet title	
Client	
Date	
Drawn by	
Notes	

Details	
Materials	
Floor	
Wall	
Colors	
Lights	
Furniture	
Decoration	
Overall mood	

PROJECT

Sheet title

Client

Date

Drawn by

Notes

Details

Materials

Floor

Wall

Colors

Lights

Furniture

Decoration

Overall mood

PROJECT

Sheet title	
Client	
Date	
Drawn by	
Notes	

Details	
Materials	
Floor	
Wall	
Colors	
Lights	
Furniture	
Decoration	
Overall mood	

PROJECT

Sheet title

Client

Date

Drawn by

Notes

Details

Materials

Floor

Wall

Colors

Lights

Furniture

Decoration

Overall mood

Mood board: Material samples/ Details/ Drafting

PROJECT

Sheet title	
Client	
Date	
Drawn by	
Notes	

Details	
Materials	
Floor	
Wall	
Colors	
Lights	
Furniture	
Decoration	
Overall mood	

Made in the USA
Columbia, SC
29 November 2020